D1738453

HIDDEN WOMEN

Frankish Splendor & Valor in Celtic Europe

the HIDDEN WOMEN *series*

Lexicus Press™

ISBN: 97-817102-941-63
LEXICUS PRESS © 2019
PALO ALTO, CALIFORNIA

LexicusPress.com
HiddenWomenBooks.com

OTHER BOOKS IN THE HIDDEN WOMEN SERIES:
A HISTORY OF EUROPE, CELTS AND FREEDOM
CELTIC BURGUNDY & EUROPE

GRAPHIC ARTIST: REMY STEINER
EDITOR: BLAIR W. STEWART
COPY EDITOR: SANDRA OHLUND
PUBLICISTS: BOJANA FAZARINC, CAM LE
ADVISORS: CAROL RUZIC, IRENE MCGHEE

HIDDEN
WOMEN

Frankish Splendor & Valor
in Celtic Europe

the HIDDEN WOMEN *series*

Lady and the Unicorn Tapestry, Museum of the Middle Ages, Paris, France

INTRODUCTION

As the curtain draws back to reveal Iron Age Europe, the concept of the Celtic civilization quietly takes shape on center stage. While invaders plundered their lands and rampaged their people, Celts steadily engineered the buildings and tended the sheep. Ironically, Europe's indigenous ones empowered the very empires that enslaved them.

50 years ago, European treasures could be viewed mainly at the Vatican and royal collections in major cities. Now, as archaeology reveals more about the originators of these splendors, new information is becoming more discernible too, even about underlying motivations. From intricately carved wine vessels to gold filigreed shoes, these finely crafted objects pay homage to male and female defenders in the grave.

Even early coinage appears to have been more a sign of respect than purchasing power. Bearing imagery of favored objects like horses and wheels, small metal coins are still being uncovered in those burial chambers that have survived unscathed. Signs of astonishing capability and productivity of Europe's Iron Age population suggest that Europe must have blossomed after the fall of Rome in the 5th century.

Those who were able to fend off attacks by empire-builders and slave hunters must have enjoyed a splendid world of peace and prosperity. Just imagine a medieval Europe at everyone's fingertips. No matter where travels led, there was always the abbey to receive the wayfarer, from far reaches of the British Isles to the former eastern realms. These fortified domains welcomed scholars, vintners, engineers, artists - and anyone who wanted to learn from them, men and women.

Once there, the newcomers joined tables with sumptuous regional specialties and lifted a chalice of local elixirs. Illuminated volumes filled domed libraries, and a nearby workshop of scribes sat in natural light to add new editions to them. Opulent gardens served as settings for meetings as well as supplying herbs and vegetables.

Woods full of mushrooms, berries and game surrounded these idyllic oases, and one could run into villagers and wayfarers there as they collected food or even quarried stone. In times of high alert, though, everyone met at the abbey for refuge. An array of castles and walled villages served as sanctuaries to fill in long distances between abbeys.

Inner spaces of the abbeys hosted an array of activities. Innovation happened here, from iron-smelting to glass-making to gilding the green leaves that graced fragile parchment pages. An integral part of the abbey and the castle continued to be the feast hall where everyone in the area joined in celebration.

Displaying the latest advances in architecture and festooned with bright banners, the great halls drew party-goers for life's auspicious occasions. Whether passerby or long-term habitant, people from near and far streamed into the halls to celebrate the nature's signposts like the winter solstice, the coming of spring and the end of the harvest. For those residing in the area, the abbey served as the place to marry and mark birthdays with special chalices and hats.

Textile and book fairs attracted visitors from the far corners; some made their way by going from abbey to abbey. Travel was sometimes prompted by specific festivities, other times by seasonal changes. When the days got shorter, it was time to move from the vineyards to the waters.

From the number of mineral spring resorts that reference the Franks and Charlemagne, it seems clear that the Frankish family led the way in developing idyllic winter retreats. Across France, Germany, Slovenia, and the Czech lands, traces of this luxurious wintering traditions can still be detected.

The cold season marked a time to slow the pace for life's more sedentary pursuits like scribing, illuminating or tasting, while warming the body in natural ways. Planning for the warmer seasons could take place in the calm, relaxed atmosphere of the baths. Dine in the great halls; sleep in the family hotel; walk in the gardens; refresh at the pavilions.

A slice of medieval life might have looked like this: the growing season has brought a good harvest in vineyards near Jeruzalem, and your son wants to marry the young woman he met at an abbey in Sticna (both in Slovenia), when he was studying astronomy. You've sent out word to your brother in Britain to meet you at the bride's family's favorite winter spot in Baden-Baden for a January wedding. Your brother and his family spend the fall and winter moving from one abbey to another, weathering storms within the walls and back on the horses in the sunshine. They help with abbey activities, make new acquaintances and learn new skills as they go.

Both bride's and groom's families end up well-represented in Baden-Baden by December in time to celebrate the solstice.

People lodge in family hotels, which are open to others in off-seasons. Since the area has operated as a winter retreat since it was first settled, larders bulge with plentiful food and libation.

The wedding takes place in the great hall. In spring the newlyweds head off to their chosen destination. They will stay close to parents later when the babies come. All of Europe belongs to them until then – they are free as the breeze.

And isn't that the way it should be.

Cluny Abbey, Cluny, France

HIDDEN WOMEN

Frankish Splendor & Valor in Celtic Europe

by Jacqueline Widmar Stewart

TABLE OF CONTENTS

CELTIC TIMELINE

1000 - 1 B.C.E.	Celts developed trade and communication networks in Europe and Britain
850 - 500 B.C.E.	Hallstatt Era, Early Iron Age in Europe
500 - 0 B.C.E.	La Tène Era, Late Iron Age
58 - 51 B.C.E.	Roman Emperor Julius Caesar's Gallic war
337	Byzantine Emperor Constantine made Christianity state religion; criminalized heresy
476	Fall of Rome
450 – 752	Merovingian governance of Francia (Clovis), including Gaul, Rhineland
529 - 534	Justinian's Code justifying slavery as law of nations that superseded natural law
650 – 700	Duchy of Carantania across Austria, Slovenia, Czech Republic
800 – 888	Carolingian governance of Francia (Charlemagne)
1095 - 1291	Crusades, main period
1100 – 1200	Resurgence of abbeys that thrived earlier with Merovingians, Carolingians
1400	Duchy of Burgundy, from Belgium to Franch-Comté

FORWARD
IN SEARCH OF FRANKS

Looking for Franks, gone for eons, sounds like an exercise in futility. Actually, it is proving quite the opposite. Traces are waiting at every turn, in plain view.

Even after the winds of war have swept the earth bare time again and again, genetics can still detect an ancient truth. Almost invariably, someone living at a long-inhabited place relates all the way back to initial settlers! People stay or leave – or they come back. Maybe not this generation, but within one or two after that, people will make their way back to an old homeland.

Accounts of origin place the Franks in the middle of Europe, in a large area known as Pannonia. According to 5th century historian Gregory de la Tours, the Franks came up from Pannonia and into the Rhineland to help throw off the chains of the Roman Empire that enslaved Europeans. Seeking signs of Franks in Pannonia and the Rhineland yields rich results; the Frankish presence still can be detected in both places.

Pannonia to the Rhineland - what did it mean to ride a horse in the 3rd century from, say, Slovenia to Germany. Crossing kingdom after kingdom, bandit upon bandit, on paths leading nowhere in a dark, nightmarish landscape fraught with peril? If science preempts fiction, this long-told tale belongs in the ashbin.

Picture, instead, roads connected and abounded with welcoming villages noted for regional specialties. There a traveler could learn, lend a hand with farming, production or maintenance and become an instant part of these small, dynamic, ever-changing communities. With an eye toward the constant threat of attack, the fortifications of these places would be of paramount concern.

Archaeological findings suggest the latter might be the more accurate depiction of pre-Christian Europe. Testing this notion can bring big rewards. If sought, the networks of old Celtic Europe can still be detected with a charm and familiarity that has endured the millennia.

First, see Europe as a whole, without political barriers or borders. Be guided by a topographical map instead. Think about the routes one would choose if coming into Europe for the first time.

DNA studies show that early settlers of Europe followed the Rhine from the north. By the Iron Age, travelers had the use of boats so that they could cross the Bosporus Straits and enter from the east with the Danube.

Even before these boats had been developed to the point that they could cross the Bosporus, the land route allowed people to come up from Africa, across the Middle East, along the northern coast of the Baltic and then follow the Rhine River south to Germany's Freiburg. Invention of watercraft short-circuited this long-way around. By crossing the Bosporus, early travelers could follow the Black Sea up to the Danube and end up in Freiburg directly from the Middle East without having to go along the northern perimeter.

At Freiburg, the Rhine wraps around and almost connects with the Danube. These two great waterways essentially form Europe's central corridor. Their sources lie within easy walking distance of each other.

When the Franks made their way from Pannonia to the Rhineland, they were following passageways well-trodden by their ancestors. The trip from Slovenia to Germany may well have been the way most travelled in the 3rd century.

Why Slovenia to Germany? The Rhineland was located on that major migratory corridor into Europe. Even before boats, the path from Africa to the Mediterranean followed the Rhine-Danube ribbon as it unfurled across the continent.

ODE TO PURPLE GOLD

Halls, pavilions, baths
Abbeys, castles, moats
Gold, salt and slate mines
Riverview and boats.

The beauty of the vineyard;
The elegance of wine;
The way the grapes gleam in the sun -
Their fragrance, rich and fine.

The age-old love of gathering
Ripe clusters in the sun
These are Frankish treasures
Remaining second to none.

FRANKISH TRACES IN PANNONIA & THE RHINELAND

Castle along the Rhine River in Germany

Frankish passages to Pannonia and back to the Rhineland

Quiet reminders keep primal place names alive - a hotel in Sopron, a Hungarian bio-refinery, an Austrian wellness spa on Stork Street in Burgenland, a Czech pathology conference in Mikulov. Distant kin whispered the words when under the rule of those trying to obliterate them. Stubbornly withstanding all the forces that have been brought to bear against it throughout time, though, some geography still clings to an age-old memory. 2500 years later, the flatlands along the eastern border between Slovenia and Hungary recall the land called Pannonia.

One glance at a topographical map snaps a realization.

Abbey gardens, St. Maur des Fossées, France

The Lakes That Once Populated Pannonia

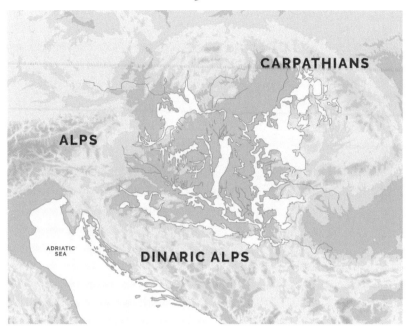

There is no mistaking Pannonia's location. Nestled in the heart of Europe, Pannonia is a giant valley ringed with natural walls. To the west, north and east, highland stones stand guard over this fertile oval. The Carpathian Mountains, the Dinaric Alps and the Alps tower over the vast valleys between them.

To see these grand central lowlands now requires a look beyond strange-shaped little bits and pieces. Despite being chopped up and called by all kinds of different names, the area now mostly consists of Slovenia, Austria, Hungary and the Czech lands.

Carantania[1] and Pannonia referred to pretty much the same area. In fact, an historian associated with Prüm Abbey that was founded under Charlemagne, Regino de Prüm,

Present Day Pannonia

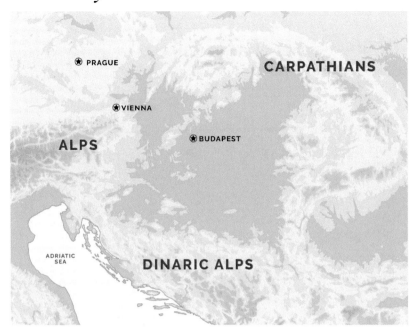

equated the two in writing his Annals of Fulda. Around the 7th century, Carantania meant the Frankish Duchy, later severed into parts that included Carinthia, Carniola, and Styria, that was then split between Austria and Slovenia.

The seat of the Duchy of Carantania quite literally was located in the middle of a field near what is now Maria Saal, not far from today's Klagenfurt (literally "ford of complaints"), but known as "Clanforte" and "Clanfurt" in Italian and Friulian respectively. Before a duke or duchess could assume the office of organizing the defense for the duchy, that person would be seated on a chair in the field to answer questions from the electorate as to whether he or she would govern fairly.[2] In the 7th century, there is evidence that the leader of Carantania was a Frank named Samo whose wife was Wendish. Please see the section on the Carolingian era for more information on the Wendish.

Celje, Slovenia

Borders today slice right through the center of old Pannonia. Austria separates the Czech lands from Slovenia; multiple languages fragment further. Despite those divisions, Vienna still maintains the aura of a capital city for Central

Europe. With its grand sister cities Prague and Budapest, these 3 cities share old secrets that bond them at the core; regardless of the political climate, central Europe treats all three cities as shared gems.

Žužemberk, Slovenia

Budapest lies southeast down the Danube river from Vienna. Across the plains to the northwest, Prague sits on the Vitava River. Vienna channeled its river away from the center, but Budapest and Prague still celebrate their riverbanks with promenades and elaborate bridges in the heart of town.

The topography in this area has changed over time. In earlier geologic ages the low-lying areas held a salt-water sea. Then in the 19th century, large-scale channelization radically changed the landscape of connecting lakes. The adjacent photo gives an idea of how eastern Europe may have looked prior to the 19th century reconfiguration of its waterways.

Grad in Slovenia

The Romans called Pannonia a Roman province once they conquered this region, but even before then it was known as Pannonia. The "ia" ending likely points to Celtic linguistic origin.

Ptuj, Slovenia

Metlika, Slovenia

Celje Tower

From Pannonia, the Danube leads right to the Rhine. The 2 rivers begin just a short portage away from each other. Not far from Freiburg the Danube begins its course runs east all the way to the Black Sea, with both Donauschingen and Furtwangen claiming the to be the starting point.

Close to the source of the Danube at nearby Magdalenenberg, a Celtic tumulus has been excavated, with findings on display at the Villigen-Schwemmingen museum.

Together the Rhine and Danube tie a neat ribbon around Europe. The Danube starts just a short portage away from the Rhine. They've almost seemed like one big river instead of two, and now more than ever since a channel recently connected them in the 1980's.

Earliest arrivals to Europe from Africa would have followed the Rhine south from the North Sea and then the Danube would have led them eastward. Once the invention of boats allowed travel across the Bosporus Straits, people could reach Europe from the Middle East directly without going along the Baltic and down the Rhine. At that point the path along the Danube would have seen much more movement west toward the Rhine. For ancient pedestrians, though, the Straits kept traffic heading primarily one way; first south on the Rhine, then east on the Danube.

Given this well-trodden Rhine-Danube corridor, the Franks' journey back to the Rhineland from Pannonia took them

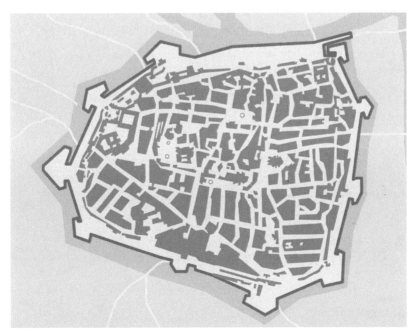

Vienna, Austria 1880

Castle in Carantania, now southern Austria

on a well-known route, and no doubt one well-populated with forbears. The further west they went, the older the settlements. Their arrival in the Rhineland must have looked like the story of the prodigal son oft-repeated, as they encountered new generations of their own kith and kin.

Another factor affected the direction of journeys along the Danube, and that involved avoiding capture. When the Roman imperial threat spread up from Rome and overtook Gaul around the 3rd century C.E., no doubt it caused those nearby to flee Roman invasion. Fleeing from invaders caused people to push further and further east along the Danube.

The 5th century would have seen a considerable shift in these patterns. Although known as the fall of the Roman Empire, a more accurate account would be a relocation of the

Empire's base of operations for the following millennium. Nonetheless, the effect on all of Europe must have been monumental at that time. Rome had lost its hold on the continent through the sacking of Rome and the return of the Rhineland and the Mosel River Valley to Celtic hands with the recapture of Worms and Trier.[3]

When the Franks and Burgundians wrested back control of Trier and Worms from the Romans, they freed Celtic Europe from the Roman threat - at least for a time and at least in part. Two observations about this transformative Celtic triumph: Imperial Rome could not have been defeated without the coordination between the Franks and Burgundians, who then went on to lead Europe as Merovingians. When the Romans suffered defeat in Rhineland strongholds and could not return to their home-base city of Rome because it had been sacked, Byzantium became the new Rome for the next 1000 years.

Žužemberk , Slovenia 1800's

Burg Hohenstein between Weisbaden and Limberg

This shift from Rome to the Middle East had tremendous impact on Europe.

During the millennium from when Rome fell in the 5th century until Constantinople was sacked in 1453, it can

be assumed that Pannonia was under ever-increasing attack
by imperialists who had relocated to what is now Turkey.
Byzantium, renamed Constantinople, sat just a short way from
where the Danube emptied into the Black Sea. The transfer
of Rome's seat of power to this eastern location lessened

vulnerability to Roman assaults in northern Europe, but opened central Europe to the Roman Imperial threat. Places that had been remote suddenly became accessible to Constantinople, and areas east along the Danube lost their safe locations.

The church state moved to Pannonia's doorstep.

As of the late 5th century, the Rhineland must have become a favored destination for refuge-seekers. Northern Europe breathed more freely under the Merovingian and Carolingian duchies, the Roman threat having been pushed back all the way to the Black Sea. But in Pannonia, the prevalence of refuge castles, moats, walls and other defensive measures - built, expanded and rebuilt over time - stand as quiet evidence of those long, tumultuous times. During the transition of Roman rule from Rome to Constantinople, people would have travelled freely back and forth from Pannonia to the Rhineland. Once the emperors had re-established their feudalistic

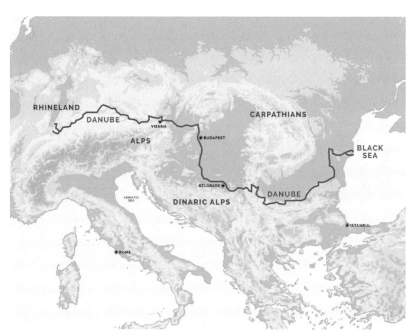

The Danube river

Nuremberg round tower

ways and began attacking from their Black Sea stronghold, however, castles, walls and moats mushroomed all over Pannonia.

Dark, steep, tower roofs harken back to times when watchtowers for attackers was a vital part of the defensive system. The multiple thermal baths and winelands within reach meant that residences of these cities could spend most of the year here without migrating too far afield. The mountains that ring the area offer cool respite from summer heat, as well as remote areas for fleeing from the enemy.

Limburg fest hall in walled town

The Iron Age settlement of Sandberg north of Vienna knew no walls. Cities of Vienna, Budapest and Prague fortified themselves mightily. When and how the threat between those times and places grew deserves much further study.

In Byzantium and eastern European areas that the Empire subsequently conquered, both the church and nobility kept slaves. Once captured and enslaved, these formerly wealthy Celts lost not only their lands, but also their rights and freedoms. Under the feudal system, only the church and nobility owned land, and they also owned the people. "Slave" and "Slav" are the same word in some languages, and at least one emperor used the terms interchangeably.[4] The top echelon overlook lands and possessions as well as the physical labors as part of their spoils of war. Thus, Celts lost their wealth, freedom and their very productive capabilities to their new masters.

What did the Celts have left? – maybe only their ability to name.

The timing and methodology of Celtic ancestors' enslavement by the church state remains beyond the reach of this inquiry. It is hoped that these subjects will be addressed by institutions capable of thoroughly investigating them.

Some indication of conquest and the time it happened may be discernible through the designation of duchy or kingdom. Duchies connoted Celtic defensive systems whereas kingdoms meant master-servant feudalism. So, for example, a map of 11th century Europe shows Duchies of Saxony, Franconia, Bohemia, Bavaria, Upper and Lower Lorraine and Spoleto, which probably meant these were Celtic-controlled lands where populations were still free and egalitarian. On the other hand, the kingdoms of Denmark, France, Burgundy, Serbia, Croatia, Hungary, Poland had probably been overtaken by feudalism at the time covered by the map.

White posts mark Celtic tumulus at Magdalenenberg, Germany

Mosel from Mariaburg

In kingdoms, it follows that all lands were owned by the nobility. Former occupants thus had been captured and made into serfs, who belonged to the nobles as chattel with the land. Enslavement also involved "droits de seigneur," that gave noble men the right to rape and torture serfs – males and females, regardless of age. Serfs had no rights of ownership; they themselves were the property of the noble estates. They could not inherit or leave an inheritance to others. As the final blow to individual liberty, the church state tightly controlled their slaves' day-to-day activities as well. Under heresy laws in effect from the 5th to 19th centuries, only religious writings and artwork were permitted; all others were punishable by death.

Along the Danube in the Rhineland

The church state overlords conquered Pannonia and the Rhineland – that's clear from church writings as well as the vestiges of the defensive systems that still can be seen, especially in these areas. Pannonia and the Rhineland were bound together for eons through DNA, pioneering and defense. For the

conqueror to enslave Celtic peoples, who had been so connected for so long by their waterways, required extremely brutal measures and enforcement. From that perspective, it is easier to understand why myriad languages, borders and "nationalities" segment the region.

MARIA, RADIGUND, MAGDALENA

Maria, Radigund, Magdalena,
These women belonged with the Franks.
What mysteries they hold may be answered
By filling in history's dark blanks.

Maria, Radigund, Magdalena,
Their names can be found everywhere,
Germany, France, and Slovenia
East realm, the west isles, even there.

All three names at the thermals,
All three with soft imagery;
They probably defended their families
With honor and great bravery.

How to pay homage to women
When your people are under the lords?
Gold shoes, diadems, jewelry
Are stolen from graves by their hordes.

So repeat their names to the children,
Name places and rivers and glades,
Attach these heroes to concepts
to withstand all of heresy's raids.

Now Maria, Radigund, Magdalena,
Are remembered on tops of the hills;
And where waters still nourish the young,
Though their roots be buried deep still.

Someday, when words such as "Celtic"
Cross our lips in the way they'd begun,
Maria, Radigund, Magdalena,
Will gain stature they once had won.

CELTIC FEMALES - EARLY LEADERS & SECULAR ABBESSES, THEN REFUGEES

Villigen, Germany; public building decoration

Celtic Females as Early Leaders & Secular Abbesses, Then Refugees

Venerated as leaders and secular abbesses in Celtic Europe, then immolated as witches, going back to an original thesis of this work, one look at the treatment of women says it all. When women are treated as chattel, any inquiry should look for oppression under the guise of religion.

Why re-examine the Merovingian and Carolingian Ages? Currently, the free world faces the same kind of abuse of women and children that ancestral Europe faced in terms of separating families and inferior treatment of women. It is crucial to understand who is behind this and why.

In the past, feudalism has been responsible for dividing and relocating families as a means to control and enslave populations. Thus, it is important to know how and when the onset of feudalism happened.[5] In Europe the early nobility – a key component of feudalism - traditionally has been ascribed to the French kings, but research is showing this to be fallacious.

Baume-les-Dames

Frankish-roofed building in Baume-les-Dames

Artifacts and reconstructions of Iron Age Celtic living reveal no evidence of overlords. The Franks were one of Europe's Celtic families. Given the fact that victors choose narratives to best suit their ends, identifying the actual beginnings of feudalism can be pivotal. The whole concept of "Germania" is looking like a figment of historian Tacitus' fantasy, with no

Place de la République & Place de la Loi signs in Baume-les-Dames

Mosel village

corroboration. The story of Merovingian and Carolingian as feudal empires is also looking fictitious.

When feudalism overtook Europe, the prevailing perspective changed from seeing others as family to regarding strangers as enemies. By its official doctrines, Christianity instills exclusivity and intolerance – only one lord; kill the pagans. It follows, then that as Christianity conquered Europe, the castles and abbeys that had offered shelter and solace became kingdoms to conquer - or be conquered by.

More and more information as to how these changes affected women is coming to light. The obvious change of the abbeys to men-only has another aspect beyond the exclusivity. The all-male bastions posed a serious threat to women, whose

protectors had to set up a system of safe houses for women. It was as though a bounty was placed on the head of every female. Celtic women went from family leaders to religious prey, as Christianity's armed monks staged a series of attacks called the Crusades.

Though the Crusades targeted specific areas, the range of terrorizing women seems to have been throughout all territories affected by Christianization. Angelsey Island in Wales, for one, was known as a

Secular windows in hall now St. Martin's church in Baume-les-Dames, France

sanctuary island where Roman legions in the first century of this era slaughtered a contingent of druids, known to have all been women. A century later, Christians followed suit by attacking the sanctuary island of Samothrace, now in Greece. Their attack coincides with the beheading of the Louvre's famed Nike of Samothrace and throwing it into the lake below. These acts, committed at two ends of the former Roman Empire by Romans and Christians a century apart, gives some sense of the breadth of this operation over space and time.

Abbey in Baume-les-Dames

Pillars in abbey, Baumes-les-Dames

Filled-in arches in abbey, Baume-les-Dames

By visiting sites with references to women in the name, one begins to see patterns forming. Often these sites are remote, and before the days of the search engines they would have been virtually impossible to find.

Within these communities one can notice, too, a repetition of familiar words and concepts. In Baumes-les-Dames, France, for example, a church now called St. Martin's is located at Place de la Loi.

One aspect to bear in mind about ancient places is what DNA studies show.[6] Almost invariably someone at the sites of early settlements links back to original migrants. Within living memory it is clear that people come back and rebuild after war – that's apparent from both world wars in this century. In a place like St. Martin's Church or the 18th century abbey in

Ceiling in hall, now St. Martin's Church, in Baume-les-Dames, France

Abbey in Baume-les-Dames, France, calling to mind Carolingian ceiling in Aachen, Germany, and St Germigyny France

Baumes-les-Dames, it is likely that these same locations have housed community gathering halls since they were first settled. It may have even been descendants of original settlers who carried forward the buildings and the designs, steadfastly rebuilding after each destruction.

The prevalence of women's refuges sends a chilling reminder of thousands upon thousands of women burned at the stake as witches in the Middle Ages. Statutory defacements have a similar impact. In the same places where men's stone and plaster faces have remained unscathed for centuries upon centuries, women's have received brutal treatment. The correlation between Christianity's conquest of Europe and the vastly

Sauer near Trier

different treatment of men and women and is hard to ignore.
After the arrival of Christianity, a disproportionate number of
women were burned at the stake, women were expelled from
abbeys because of their gender and there was proliferation of
refuges for women, as well as an onslaught of physical abuse and
defacement of female statues.

One of the places hardest hit historically by mass murders of women is the Rhineland.

To understand the importance of the Rhineland to Celtic Europe, it helps to look at the geography and some key names. Trier is located strategically on the Mosel, before it feeds into the Rhine, which then joins the Main River. Just barely inside Germany, it also lies close to the borders of Luxemburg Belgium and France, a sure sign of its importance since borders have been used in the past as an effective means of dividing people.

Frankish towers, Fulda, Germany

Tours, France

Towers, Würzburg, Germany

Along both the Rhine and the Mosel are some of the world's best wine producing areas, and Celts – men and women - are well-known for their affinity for wine.[7] Examples spread wide across Europe – the wine cellar at Asparn-an-der-Zaya, Austria's reconstructed village, the wine amphora shards used as construction fill at Bibracte, France, the multitude of wine amphora found near Bourges, France, the numerous vessels for mixing wine (situla) found near Novo mesto, Slovenia.[8]

Trier also stands as a silent reminder of the defeat of Roman occupiers who wrested control from the Celts who had settled there centuries before. Reportedly, Julius Caesar "subdued" the Treveri, the family associated with Treves, the Celtic name for Trier, during the 8 years between 58 and 50 B.C.E. A non-victor's description of those years would involve subjugation and enslavement of the Celts by the Romans.

Crypt in Michaelskirche, Fulda, Germany

Square tower, Wurzburg, Germany

Towers, Würzburg, Germany

Hydrology, Bamberg, Germany

The name of the Alemanni family is frequently associated with the Rhineland and with the first Merovingian leader Clovis, as discussed further below; thus there is good reason for the assumption that the Alemanni

are a Celtic family, even though that assumption conflicts with the victor's version of history. The staying power of the Alemanni is apparent from the fact that the two names by which they are known still are recognizable in Europe

Building over the river, Bamberg, Germany

today. The French refer to all inhabitants of the Republic of Germany as "Allemands." The other name for the Alemanni – Schwabia – is a region in Bavaria that used to be a duchy, a high-level Celtic administrative district for calling up troops. The reasons for this assumption are discussed more fully later in this book.

Trier also is one of the 4 places where women were accused of being witches and burned at the stake in the greatest numbers. The other 3 cities: Fulda, Würzburg and Bamberg.

Fulda was one of the 4 abbeys in the Odenwald said to have been founded by Charlemagne himself, and still contains a Merovingian crypt in a building with distinctively Frankish-looking black slate-roofed towers. High walls point to a more extensive defensive system in the past. Fulda sheltered

Gilded carvings of women and natural motifs in Bamberg

11th century festive hall, now dom, Bamberg, Germany

Natural motifs ceiling, feather, white stones, Bamberg, Germany

women in the late Middle Ages, reflecting the defensive measures that were broadly taken against the church state's witch-burning campaigns.

One that used to hold a Bronze Age refuge castle, Würzburg's heavily fortified Marienberg now stands at the top of the hill. Würzburg is said to have been populated by Alemanni and Franks and the seat of a Merovingian duchy. It also contains an area just down from the fortress known as "Frauenland."

Bamberg lies on the river Regnitz close to confluence with the Main River, but also equidistant from the Rhine and Danube, with a connecting Rhine-Main-Danube channel now running right through it.[9] Archeological research has uncovered massive walls and a moat from the 10th century that had protected the abbey on the top of the hill, while the main part of the town clustered on the river's edge.

Rhine, Main & Mosel Rivers

1000 women are estimated to have been killed as witches in the 17th century in these 4 cities alone.

For a place that gives rare insight into what refuges for women might have been, consider the city of Quedlinburg. This beautiful town full of half-timbered houses and vibrant market square, lies just to the east of the infamous Hartz Mountains. In the Middle Ages, the church accused the Harz of harboring witches, and some names still bear reference to those times, like "Tierpark Hexendanzplatz," for example, which means Animal Park – where the witches dance."

Quedlinburbg white & black towered house

Quedlinburg house fronts

A trip into the Hartz yields quite a different impression than the old notions of witch-infested heights, however. From all appearances, theses warm, gracious, mountain dwellers thrive on hiking their trails among the charming villages scattered throughout the hills. Vestiges of ancient festive halls can also still be seen in the town and in the heights.

Quedlinburg's secular abbey sheltered women.

With this in mind, the shield for Quedlinburg is open to interpretation. In the Iron Age, shields served to identify those in battle with others on the same side. Two places in particular lead to that supposition. Asparn-an-der-Zaya, now north of Vienna, Austria, exhibits shield raised high above the solemn enclosure that honors the defenders. In Kortrijk,

Quedlinburg vine-covered building

Belgium, brightly colored panels show elegantly dressed figures – men and women – adorned with gold, and with their brightly colored shields prominently in view.

Initially, the use of shields as identification most likely started with families. By the time those in Quedlinburg were using shields in the Middle Ages, the elements on this shield look as though they were associated with the activities, probably associated with the women of the refuge abbey. Two possibilities for the meaning of the two paddles with blunted tips seem plausible - frosting spreaders or plaster smoothers.

Organizing according to practical abilities already mattered 2000 years ago – this is apparent from the Iron Age Celtic settlement at Titelberg in Luxemburg. There the living quarters were arranged according to occupation, well before the

Woman's head over the window in Quedlinberg

guilds gained prominence in the later Middle Ages. One other observation about the paddles on the Quedlinburg shield would be this. Notice the beautifully crafted handles, reflecting the importance of aesthetics that broadly affected aspects of Celtic life.

On a remote mountaintop in Austria, which would have been known as ancient Pannonia or 7th century Carantania, Frauenstein castle evinces characteristics of a women's refuge by name and location. A local hiking map of the area spots numerous safe houses tucked away into this region. Just outside Wiesbaden a rectangular tower stands guard on top of a promontory so steep that it cuts the sky like a knife. Accessible from only one direction, it belonged to a castle that was also called Frauenstein. Another place named Frauenstein used to house a castle in Germany on the border of the Czech Republic in the Eastern Ore Mountains.

Quedlinburg stair with roofed entry

Quedlinburg shield

Another example of an abbey beautifully portraying women in a way like Quedlinburg does - decorated with gold and with heads held high - occurs in Eichstatt in a hall now known as Marienkirche. To the contrary, the females gracing this hall are celebrated with golden diadems and wrapped in gold leaf. What

Quedlinburg - wolf broke through the wall

The way to the Refuge Castle in Frauenstein, Austria

Refuge Castle in Frauenstein, Austria

was likely a safe house for women, the building on Frauenberg still sits on top of the town's hill. Inside, some Christian trappings have obviously been added to statues of the women, like Abbess Walpurgis for example.

Walpurgis was an abbess in the 8th century, associated with Whitby Abbey in England. Each fall Walpurgisnacht is still widely celebrated with bonfires in northern and central Europe in the Netherlands, Germany, the Czech Republic, Slovenia, Sweden, Lithuania, Latvia, Finland, and Estonia. According to some reports, she was buried at Heidenheim – literally "heathen home" and later her remains were transferred to Eichstatt, Germany.[10]

Head of gilded woman gilded in Marienkirche in Eichstatt

Also portrayed in the Frauenberg hall is Notburga, who is said to have been either from the 8th or 13th century, according to different sources. Shown with a scythe and floral wreath on her head, a sheaf of grain, a basket of cheese and keys, a portrait of her graces the church on Lake Bled's island in Slovenia. Notburga

Statue of Abbess Walpurga in Kirchehrenbach, Germany. Note the spiral staff

is said to have been the daughter of Dagobert I, the last of the Merovingian leaders, and associated with Cologne, Germany, known for its population of Saline Franks, who originated the Salic law codes. She's also venerated in Baden, Germany, a thermal spa resort.

Abbess Stilla of Abenberg, a town in Middle Franconia

Abbess Notburga, as shown in Bled, Slovenia

Woman in gold with golden goblet. Sankt Leonhard, Austria.

A third woman honored with a statue in Frauenberg is Stilla, who stands holding flowers, an open book and what was probably a towered festive hall. She is associated with Abenberg, on the north edge of the Frankish lake district, lying between the Frankish Hills to the north and the Frankish Alps to the south and west.[11] This area was closely tied to Würzburg and Nurnberg, where thousands of women were burned at the stake by the church state in the Middle Ages. Since the Roman Catholic Church canonized her as a saint in the 13th century, it is likely that she actually lived several centuries earlier, as in the case of Notburga.

Gilded woman holding castle, Sankt Leonhard, Austria

Other places named Frauenberg also occur in what is now Styria, Austria, the former Carantania (Pannonia), where what was probably once a festive hall still stands. In the Moselle region in northeastern France, the ruins of a castle still exist, just on the border with Germany.

Signs of refuges for women also can be found in the old Pannonia, also known as 7th century Carantania. In areas that contain a name with a "saint" later added to it, or a Celtic-style descriptive place name, it is sometimes possible to find evidence of traditionally Celtic practices. Here, "Leonhard" may well come from "Lion heart," and be a reference to Richard the Lion-hearted. The Lion has been portrayed as a symbol for courage across Celtic culture.

Chandelier based on spirals in Sankt Leonard, Austria

Castle ruins. Sankt Leonhard, Austria

The older the building that now houses a church, the more likely the chance to find something like this exquisite, gilded female warrior from Bad Sankt Leonhard in Lavanttal, in the district of Wolfsberg, in Carinthia, Austria. In the same

hall, a woman wearing a gilded red crown, is likely honored here as a fallen defender of the castle she holds in one hand. In her other hand she carries a red book with a cross on it. The symbol of the even-spoked cross probably derives from the 8-spoked

Probable former festive hall on Sankt Leonhard, Austria

wheel, as evidenced by the Celtic cross. Another woman holding a castle is similarly honored.

In France a road known as "Chemin des Dames" lies a handful of miles away from Vauclair Abbey, said to have been

founded by 12th century Bernard de Clairvaux of Burgundy. In nearby Laon cathedral, a probable former festive hall, a mother-and-child statue of black marble with golden diadem, has managed to survive, although the son's arm is shattered.

Laon, France

The statuary outside has not fared as well: 4 graceful statuesque women stand beheaded in their niches, and even two placed high above the door have been vandalized. It is also interesting to imagine how lively the hall might once have appeared before the removal of color as well as the defacing of female statues. Although the interior walls are devoid of color and many of the arches have been walled in, it is possible to gain a sense of its more colorful and open past through the model on display. An additional female hero is honored at Laon, although her identification is somewhat obscured. Joan of Arc stands with her banner and

Laon, France

Model of former hall in Laon, France

Keltenwelt, Austria

boyish haircut, apparently trying to draw as little attention to herself as possible.

In what is now Austria, near the Karawanka (Celtic word) tunnel, a new archeological site adds to understanding both the place and plight of women in Celtic – and Christian - culture. Interpretation is needed here to comprehend the outsized wood statue of a woman standing on a pile of rock and animal skeleton head.

Joan of Arc

93

TWO HEADS OF THE FRANKISH STATE

Clovis and Charlemagne,
Two Frankish leaders,
Led Francia after Rome's fall:
Clovis 5th century, Charlemagne 8-9th.

Clovis served as first Merovingian
With Clothilde, his Burgundian wife.
Both Charlemagne's sister and mother
Founded abbeys in France and Germany.

Culture flourished under their lead,
Trade connected the lands;
Building blossomed; learning spread;
Parks and gardens graced the domain.

Documentation is scarce;
Most traces have been destroyed.
The rocks and rills hold memories still
Of these fair and fruitful times.

FRANKS CLOVIS & CHARLEMAGNE, GUARDS OF CELTIC CULTURE

Landesmuseum, Stuttgart, Germany

Franks Clovis and Charlemagne, Guards of Celtic Culture in Merovingian and Carolingian Eras

This period has been referenced as the Darkening Ages, and misinformation still plays a key role in keeping the medieval period dark.[12] Until the 15th century when the last holdouts in Belgium fell to the Hapsburg Empire, it is difficult to determine who was flying under what flags. Deception and confusion play leading roles in Europe's past, and they remain equally problematic in trying to decipher what happened when and where.

Twilight. Keltenwelt, Austria

This juncture calls for a change of voice. I want to speak directly to you, my Reader, because I feel you will benefit from my own personal experiences.

For me, the study of history has been a kaleidescope. Let me offer you a couple of examples. When I went to look at Worms for myself, to see the famous old German city that had been so important to the Roman Empire, I found that the city's famous German heroic epic was not German, but Burgundian. Not only that, it was the Burgundian account of a battle against the Romans, and initially not told in the German language at all.

When I visited Aachen the first time as a college student, we were shown the renowned hall where Charlemagne was crowned king – it was the seminal visit of the whole trip. Now, common convention says that Charlemagne was crowned in Rome – and there's barely a whisper of even Charlemagne's name in Aachen.

In looking at a broader historic and archeological record, I can see that the Roman Catholic Church has designated as its own saints those Celtic abbesses who founded Celtic abbeys.[13] This is true from Britain to Pannonia - as well as for warriors like Joan of Arc who defended against feudal attacks.

From my studies of languages, I can see manipulation in both the words and structure of languages; this is an area that cries out for further study.

By seeing the care and respect shown to male and female defenders in Iron Age burial chambers, and by seeing the extreme measures that Europe's peoples had to take to protect themselves, I sense a specter of slavery that loomed ever larger for our ancestors until they were restrained by the violence and brutality that we still see at work today.

Recently we found a mischaracterization of the Carolingian Era – by about 800 years. What was billed as a Carolingian reconstruction looked much more like the Iron Age in Messkirch, Germany. I consider this as an attempt to cast medieval Europe as barbaric in order to hide the church-state's enslavement of Celts.

The further I step back and look at these and other striking inconsistencies, the more they fall into line with a few basic assumptions. The past becomes much clearer by bearing these basics in mind:

- Europe has been populated by essentially the same people, whether Bronze Age, Iron Age, or the Modern Age.

- Europe was connected in the Celtic era before it was divided by Imperialism.

- The people in Europe were free before they were enslaved by feudalism.

- Today's forced separations of families and escalations of weapons of mass destruction are carry-overs from imperial feudalism. They are another form of the brutality and violence that dictators use to enslave populations. For the sake of future generations, we must stop these atrocities once and for all.

Namur citadel tower

To imagine the Merovingian Age, it helps to remember the magnificent stone castle that stands guard over the Meuse River in Namur, Belgium, or the stately towers, walls and moat of the one on the Meuse in Metz, Germany. From these two examples alone, it is easy to see that the Celts in the 5th to 8th

centuries became proficient with rounded stone towers and massive earth- and waterworks.

It stands to reason, then, that the round Merovingian towers in St. Maur des Fossés just outside of Paris, the one in Compiègne near the Vivenel Museum indicate the presence of

St-Maur-des-Fossées, France

Franks in those places in those times. Those in southern France and the Baltic in Germany and Poland do too. Just as Burgundian elements can be seen all over Europe (as referenced in *Celtic Burgundy & Europe*, the 2nd book in this *Hidden Women* series), so can the Frankish. The Frankish and Burgundian elements of Celtic culture merge in the Merovingian Era, just as the families of wife Clothilde and husband Clovis and did in marriage.

Thus, the Franks play a leading role in this era of history. Clovis, the first Merovingian leader, is said to have been Frankish, and there is no apparent reason to think otherwise. The claimed conversion to Christianity and subsequent supposed baptism at the cathedral in Reims, though, go beyond the realm of possibility.

Crowning of Clovis, from Burgundische Tapisserien

A 15th century tapestry tells a different story.

This tapestry, woven some 1000 years after Clovis had lived, portrays the crowning of Clovis. Upon closer examination, a backdrop of bishops seems to be holding up a grey, lifeless figure.

The meaning of this tapestry carries far-ranging implications. Christianity converted resident populations by subjugation and the sword. Empires maintained the state religion by force and subsumed the culture of the conquered, especially after the 12th century. An idea of how this was accomplished can be garnered through the depiction of Clovis' corpse being propped up by the bishops.

Clovis' conversion to Christianity seems as unlikely as Vercingetorix' embracing the enemy that starved out thousands of his people at Alesia, or Julius Caesar suddenly becoming a Celt. The Celts had seen Rome annex and enslave southern Gaul; they knew that Julius Caesar took Vercingetorix back to Rome and dragged him behind a chariot in the coliseum after he had tried to trade his life for the freedom of the women and children starving in Alesia. Julius Caesar bragged about slaughtering Celts, about slaying women and children migrating from one place to another – his words have controlled the narrative for the past 2000 years.

What reason would there be for Roman Catholic bishops to crown a corpse king, and how likely is it that this could happen? The Roman Empire built its reputation on ruthlessness and terror; as its successors, the Christian conquerors used Rome's infrastructure in Europe. Latin had been devised as the Roman language, although it was probably never the spoken language anywhere. The Roman Catholic church's edicts were enforced by the Roman legal system and carried out in every parish by Rome's chosen delegates.

Stepping into the shoes of Roman bishops following Clovis defeat at Tolbiac might shed some light. Imagine a scenario that would be far more likely to have happened than a Merovingian Frank like Clovis converting to the enemy's religion.[14] Here's one idea of what a de-briefing among bishops might have been.

OVER CLOVIS' DEAD BODY

"Now that we've shown how brutal we can be -
with our raping and slaying spectacles -
we have succeeded in traumatizing the Celts.
Problem is, we're the outsiders.
As soon as we're gone, they're back to their ways.
We need a way to sustain their subservience,
to keep them paying tribute,
even when we turn our backs."

"Remember Vercingetorix at Alesia a few centuries ago?
Julius Caesar took that Celtic leader back to Rome and
dragged him behind a chariot in the coliseum.
That provided grisly fanfare -
Terrified everyone in Gaul -
but it made them fight us with more ferocity too.

We've performed every heinous act we can conceive,
And they're becoming inured to it.
We've forced whole families to watch
while we systematically
And painfully slowly torture their offspring
Starting with the youngest and worked our way up
Without ever flinching.

The theater of slaughter and rape has become routine for us.
We need to devise something more,
Something less detectable but lasting."

"We need to lull them into submission,
And do it surreptitiously
so they'll obey without a struggle –
without even knowing it's happening.

Let's see. We need to hook into something
that's important to them.

Besides family, where's their
greatest vulnerability? What matters to them?
Where do they direct
their attention and wealth?"

"Here's a thought.
They idolize their heroes.
At death, they decorate the corpses
with the finest golden diadems,
Torques, even filigreed shoes."

"Well now, there's a thought.
Clovis, leader of the Franks is dead, yes,
but we've got the body.
Now they can't bury him with all that gold
and honor him as a fallen defender."

"Ok. Here's how we take it to another level.
Let's make that corpse sing for us.

If they have such reverence for dead warriors,
It will overwhelm them to see their lifeless leader
Telling them to do our bidding."

"If Clovis tells them to do what we say, they'll listen.
They don't need to know he's dead.
We'll prop him up and give him our symbols of power
The scepter, the crown.
We'll make him king Clovis, feudal ruler.

Illuminations from Burgundische Tapisseriern likely showing women in forced baptism

They'll never know it's a sham.
We'll put him far enough away, and
Prop him up high on his seat,
With all the imperial trappings."

"We bishops will be the ventriloquists,
the power behind Clovis' throne."

In addition to the tapestry on Clovis' questionable coronation, there's another tapestry from the 15th century that also sheds light on an early Christian practice.[15] Christianity and kingdoms appear to have been fused together in those days. The language of Christianity talks in terms of kingdom and obedience to the king – "thy kingdom come, thy will be done on earth as it is in heaven." Adherents to Christianity pray for an eternal dictatorship during which they will praise their masters throughout their servitude.

Who voluntarily submits to involuntary servitude? What is going on here?

A second scene from Clovis' time in around the 5th century can shed some light on this conundrum. A universal truism is that when your family is threatened, their well-being comes first. This explains why those who stayed in Europe under repressive regimes served them without looking left or right. It was the only way they survived.

This scene shows naked people being ushered to a font in a pavilion, while outside armed horsemen try to keep a frenzied crowd at bay.[16] In its title, it portrays the Alemani, whom the Romans identify as a Germanic tribe (that is being shown more, and more, to have been a myth of their own making.[17] Likely, the Alemani were another Celtic family in the Rhineland.

The caption on the tapestry reads "How the king discomfited the Alemani." From Roman to Byzantine, all of the empires imposed a feudal master-servant system in the areas they controlled. The title could as easily read "How the Romans subjugated the Alemani Celts."

This notion is supported further by the fact that the closely related "Allemands" in French means "Germans." The newer German language deviates substantially with "Die Deutsche"

Applying the theory that Old Frankish and thus modern French derives from old Celtic languages, the reference to the people living along the Rhine as "Alemani" would be an older Celtic form.

The victor's version of history tells that Clovis the Frank defeated the Alemani at Tolbiac. This assertion appears highly unlikely on its face. Evidence shows that the Alemani lived in the Rhineland, along the Burgundians and Franks.

Detail of Burgundische Tapisseriern

The Celts came to each other's aid, as when Vercingetorix came from Auvergne to help the Burgundians surrounded by Romans at Alesia, and the Franks and Burgundians ruling together as a married couple after defeating the Romans at Trier and Worms.

Even looking at a photograph of the tapestry 500 years later sends a chill up the spine. Clearly the message is subservience, meant to be disturbing to those having to watch and as well as those reporting the acts to others. Those in the pavilion have been stripped naked and are being herded, with eyes closed and hands clasped, up to a receptacle of water that looks very much like a modern baptismal font.

Like parading around the corpse of warrior hero Clovis, the immersion into water as part of what may well be a death or rape ritual links water - one of the most cherished elements of Celtic life – to death. The horrific message is unmistakable: just watch what happens if you disobey. As an added blow, well-dressed women are being used to carry out these unspeakable acts.

To put these tapestries into the context of the Rhineland, some attention should be given to the location of Trier. The Franks reclaimed this city from the Romans, and it sits on the Mosel River that then runs into the Rhine River. Just south of where the Mosel joins the Rhine, the Main River also flows into the Rhine. A billboard-like signal that this area has Frankish roots comes from the biggest and busiest city in this area, Frankfurt, or Frankish ford. The fact that this name has been able to withstand centuries of renaming struggles testifies to its significance.

An appellation like "The Celtic Union" or "Federation" may fit as a description for the second half of the first millennium, perhaps, but not the "Frankish Empire". Though Charlemagne is lauded in Latin texts as emperor, his Frankish background would have repelled even the idea of enslaving others. Considerable evidence indicates that the Franks adhered to the Celtic culture, and Charlemagne's ancestors had fought to preserve it against Roman invasions.

Charlemagne, his mother and sisters all established abbeys, traces of which sometimes still can be discerned. From the design and fortifications, the abbeys appear to have served both academic and production purposes as well as sanctuary during attacks. Perhaps the greatest sign of his importance, however, lies in the preservation of his memory. It cannot be measured in terms of statuary or books, since art and literature from his era have been essentially obliterated. It comes in a more organic way, those who keep his name alive.

The name Charlemagne evokes benevolence and prosperity, a leader who presided over Europe's finest moment. It rises to the top of idyllic periods, when the bounty of the land was shared by all, not hoarded in the coffers of a few overlords. The time shines as one when women worked alongside men and were not derided as the gates of hell, a time when women founded and ran abbeys that were roughly the equivalent of our present-day university campuses.

Charlemagne and hall

Notions about Charlemagne derive primarily from his biographer Einhard, who is credited with a writing in German, as recorded in the Royal Frankish Annuls. According to the Roman Catholic Church's accounts, Charlemagne converted to Christianity and spread religion by sword across Europe.

These accounts raise several red flags, however. There is no evidence that Charlemagne abandoned his commitment to family, women and nature to embrace Roman imperialism; Charlemagne's precursors notoriously battled to the death against Rome's constant attacks and enslavements of the Celtic people. The lack of any robust endorsement by religion further substantiates this position. If Charlemagne had been Christianity's most prestigious convert, he would have been hailed as their poster child and touted throughout Europe. To the contrary, Charlemagne's memory has all but been erased, especially if contrasted with, say, the publicity of the pope.

The area led by Charlemagne has been referenced as an empire, along with other designations such as "royal" and "court." Based on the theory that Franks belonged to the Celtic culture, though, Charlemagne the Frank would have led defensive efforts to fend off invading Roman legions. One major difference between the tactics of Celts and Romans comes across as the tolerance for brutality. In their own writings, Romans like Julius Caesar obviously relished slaughtering women and children by the thousands as an offensive strategy. The Celts, as Europe's resident populations, are known for their defensive measures when under siege, and fierce attacking their attackers.

Moreover, cornerstones of Europe's feudal system line up with Roman practices, not Celtic ones. From the layout of their villages alone, it is apparent that Roman males presided in outsize villas, while their slaves and underlings lived in humble circumstances. Celts, on the other hand, inhabited relatively same-sized housing, but gathered in the communal hall for meals, community projects and celebrations.With their pan-European networks, Celts moved about freely and without boundaries before the onset of the Roman Empire and, later, the borders imposed by feudal lords to restrict the movements of their subjects.

Another suspicious part of the Charlemagne story concerns the "royal" Frankish annuls. The very words constitute a contradiction in terms, and cast into doubt the reliability of writings attributed to Charlemagne's biographer. For reasons set out in the first two books in this series, the Celtic Franks adhered to egalitarian principles. Royalty implies a feudal system of lords, kings and aristocracy, which diametrically opposed the Celtic way of life.

The fact that Einhard's writing supposedly used the German language also raised issues of validity. Charlemagne's domain would have communicated in old Frankish, a Celtic tongue that preceded today's French language. According to historians - whose job was to praise the conquerors - the territory under Charlemagne's purview was divided into West, Middle and East realms (hence names like Ost-Reich, or Österreich). According to conventional wisdom, the East Realm switched its language to German when one of Charlemagne's grandsons married a German-speaking woman who wanted the region to speak her language. That is used to explain why two Slavic-speaking areas like the Czech lands and Slovenia are divided by a swath of German-speaking Austria. Ethnic origin obviously has nothing to do with the fact that Germany and Austria became German-speaking.

Furthermore, the changeover to German-speaking in the former Eastern Empire is not supposed to have taken place until the alleged division by Charlemagne grandsons two generations later. Attribution of German-speaking to him is, thus, an anachronism; as a contemporary to Charlemagne, Einhard would have lived two generations before the grandsons. Charlemagne's realm – and presumably the scholars in it – would have spoken Frankish. It stands to reasons that division by language later occurred under the conquerors as a means to keep people from organizing against their domination.

It seems indisputable that language has been imposed involuntarily upon populations because language doesn't change at the border by itself. Splintering people into myriad languages fractionalizes the collective memory. With that in mind, even seemingly subtle changes in Charlemagne, like Charles the Great, Karl der Grosse, Carol, Karel and Carl, can cause confusion and uncertainty.

Students are taught to spell exactly, and that even small discrepancies change meaning. Less often do they learn to look for commonalities despite slight variations, or, more broadly, that language has been used to recraft history. That said, internet search engines are opening up new research possibilities by expanding spelling variations.

Here's one other point about language before looking more closely at the name Charlemagne. Imagine what life would be like under a regime so repressive that any non-religious utterance, written or oral, is punishable by death. It would have been difficult to enforce these kinds of restrictions at all times everywhere in Europe, but for about 1400 years the church's heresy laws were enforceable by the Roman legal system.

Karlovy Vary the solremn rites of marriage

Women as healers in Karlovy Vary

Karlovy Vary and the park around the pavilions

In such circumstances, it is likely that a parent would not share knowledge with the children because to do so would put them in risk of their lives. How, then, do you pass along any information about what you know?

Names.

Spelling does not matter; it's all in the sound.

Karlovy Vary. Statue in the pavilions

The Baths at Karlovy Vary

The pavilions of Karlovy Vary

A few of the place names that remember Charlemagne include Karlsbad, Karlsruhe, Karlstein am Main, Karlsplatz in several cities like Vienna and Munich, the octagonal Karlskirche in Vienna that bears similarities of design with other Carolingian halls.

Perhaps the greatest tribute to Charlemagne remains vibrant, elegant and splendid just across the German border in what is now the Czech Republic: Karlovy Vary. There, a grand,

In Karlovy Vary Women as Pillars

columnaded pavilion parallels the river that flows gently through the heart of the thermal bath resort. Under the shelter of towering, intricately carved ceilings in majestic white soaring spaces, numerous fonts spring forth with hot mineral waters for all to share. Nearby kiosks carry little painted china cups with built-in straws.

Widening the circle, here are a few of the places associated with the Carolingians: in France - St. Germigny-des-Près; in Germany - Aachen, Fulda, Lorsch, Carolinenfield, Johannisberg Abbey.

Charlemagne's Officer Roland

A name that comes to the fore in the era of Charlemagne, Roland is most notable for the early piece of literature written in old French called La Chanson de Roland, or the Song of Roland. Long reputed to be one of the first major works in the old French language.

The case of Roland gives a rare chance to better understand how the Christian conquest of Europe worked. Following the usual pattern, the conqueror removes existing communication networks of the resident population by burning books and commandeers the language by assigning different meaning to the words. The Chanson de Roland does just that. It takes a venerated name from the Celtic past – a known defender in Charlemagne's era – and, from the very first words, inserts the threat of death and atrocity into the familiar hero's tale.

Christianity destroyed writing in the native language as a matter of course in its conquests, by burning books and proscribing in heresy laws all that was not in keeping with its religious dictates. This happened in Mexico, in the Philippines, and in Egypt when Cyril notoriously burned the library of Alexandria. Cyril went one step further, in what probably was common operating procedure for overtaking communication. Acting as monks of the Byzantine Empire in the 9th century, he and his brother Methodius devised not only another language, but even a new script for it - in addition to the older Greek and newer Roman-created Latin.

It comes as no surprise that the story of Roland appeared in a language different than the one spoken at the time of the action some 300 years earlier, written in the 12th about the 9th.

It also comes as no surprise that the main

Windischheim, Germany, statue of Charlemagne"s Roland

Detail of Roland in Quelinburg

thrust of the first words are to strike fear and death into the
hearts of the subjugated peoples.

On page one, the Chanson de Roland, calls into question
its own legitimacy as an authentic literary work. The line reads:
*"Let us send the sons of our own wives. It is far better that they should
lose their heads than that we should lose our honor and our dignity and
be reduced to beggary."*

Sending sons to die would have been reprehensible to
Celts, who prized and protected their children. The few artifacts
that remain from those times strongly support this conclusion.

The test of sacrificing sons goes all the way back to Abraham – *"Will you sacrifice your son for me?"* The story of Christ goes further – a god actually offering his own son as a human sacrifice. (Never mind that the son allegedly came back to life; the guilt remains). Here, in an account supposedly derived from the 9th century, (but written some 300 years later) feudalistic lords are purportedly bartering with the lives of their people and with their pledges of loyalty and conversion to Christianity.

As a Frankish Celt, there is no likelihood that Charlemagne would trade women and children into the slavery of medieval Christianity. As Europe's resident population, the Celts fought relentlessly against Roman – and Christian - conquest and enslavement. Viewed from that perspective, these words are those that a conqueror-enslaver would say to cause their captives to bow down and stay submissive. This is the same rhetoric that gives rise to a statue of a mother holding her dead son. The mention of sacrificing sons is meant to paralyze the audience with fear and dread, and to send the message that death awaits those who fail to comply with the master's orders.

The concept of proving loyalty by showing a willingness to sacrifice one's own son should be construed as a sign of enslavement. The suggestion of killing one's own children needs to strike an ear-shattering bell for anyone who hears it. The notion of "civilization" or "civility" cannot co-exist with infanticide.

In Quedlinburg, mentioned above, the name Roland is displayed with medieval-style signage and a depiction of the quintessential knight.

Roland is associated with another key name from the Middle Ages, the Wendish. His statue stands on the main square of Bad Wendsheim in Germany's greater Rhineland. In that thermal-springs health town full of half-timbered houses, there is also a reconstruction of a medieval Frankish village named Franken Therma. It is highly unlikely that associations such as these happen by chance.

The Wendish family, in a variety of different spellings, plays a part in the story of 7th century Central Europe's Samo of Carantania, whose wife has been identified as Wendish. The extended family of the Counts of Celje in 14th century Slovenia reputedly included a Wendish branch. As in so many places bearing Frankish influence, the multi-tiered, beautifully decorated, inner courtyard galleries exhibit a commonality of design.

Aachen thermal baths

Franken Park, Wendischeim

There's a Windesheim in Austria and the Netherlands, too and a Windisch-Bleiberg in Austria. Windisch in Switzerland refers to a munipality in the district of Brugg, Aargau Canton. Wendisch-Evern sits just south of Lüneburg in the former East Germany. The Wendisch Rietz is near a nature park just south of Berlin. The list goes on. In these instances, Google proves invaluable in bridging linguistic gaps that may well have been created intentionally.

Like the Cathars and Lithuanians that were also the objects of Christian Crusades, the Wendish were attacked by warrior monks as part of a Crusade against them in the 12th century. The German word for Crusade, "Wendenkreuzzug", literally means "holy war." An account by a Helmold of Bassau states that "there was no mention of Christianity, but only of money,"[18] an observation that evokes the old Roman ways of exacting tribute.

Aachen interior, octagon from Charlemagne's time

The Crusades that were directed against specific areas in Europe left a devastation that can still be felt today, some 9 centuries later. Untold numbers of people were slaughtered in the name of Christianity in Mecklenburg and Pomerania, beautiful

lake-filled lands near the Baltic Sea in what is now Germany and Poland. These lands still evince scars from those times. Reminiscent of Flanders Fields' poppies, the bright orange flowers here revive recollections from inside the earth. Like France's

Champagne Region and concentration camps from any war, chilling memories of atrocities committed on those lands seem to hang in the air and cannot be dispelled.

Frankish and Burgundian, Merovingian and Carolingian – the intertwining of these 4 families and eras throughout Europe evidence how fully ingrained they were in the landscape of the times – and how much they reflect the Celtic life then. If trappings from the Merovingian epoch seem solid and charming with their big, bold rounded towers and shallow conical roofs, then the hallmarks of the Carolingian Age rise above the earth as lofty, elegant silhouettes.

With its domed, arched-windowed octagon, Aachen comes to mind as the epitome of Carolingian grace and style. Also known as Aix-la-Chappelle, and Bad Aachen, this town drew early travelers because it offered year-round natural

Aachen, octagon from Charlemagne's time

Aachen, interior of halls

heating with its thermal springs, now developed into an extensive, modern resort called Carolus Therme. The town is also strategically located, as evidenced by its close proximity to Belgian and Netherlands borders. Bad Aachen reputedly counted as Charlemagne's favorite place; it is said that 31 Holy Roman feudal lords were later crowned there.

Though the building most associated with Charlemagne's era has been altered, still the octagonal part is attributed to his tenure. Even from the scant vestiges of structures that remain intact, it is still possible to discern favored motifs that might have been keep alive rather than revised. Gilded, ornate and use of a deep persimmon color come forth as distinctive attributes in Prüm that can also be

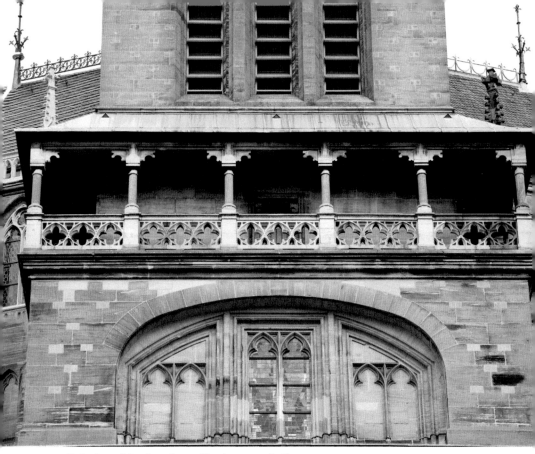

Exterior of Aachen from Charlemagne's time

seen in other places in Europe, sometimes surprisingly like Ljubljana, Slovenia.

Another feature is the use of two large spirals that act almost as quotation marks on the roof just as the wall façade begins to narrow. Similarities can be seen at Laval Abbey in Monthermé, France, at Memmingen and Hamelin, Germany.

This supposition arises from a bit of information gained in Melrose Abbey in Scotland. Although built somewhat later than the Carolingian Era, around the 12th century, information at the abbey credited the architect Morrow. What would that name not be spelled Morrow rather than the "French" spelling? It's a clue worth investigating.

Prüm Abbey sheilds and gold

Prüm Abbey hall

Prüm Abbey, woman holding a pillar

Another hypothesis derives from the material that enabled the steep spires and gave a deep, dark beauty to the swords piercing the skies. In Karolinenfield – which may well mark the area where the Empire extinguished the life of Charlemagne - and in neighboring Berleburg, it is hard not to notice the distinctive, particular appearance of the buildings. Overlapping scallops of slate not only roof these structures, but form the vertical walls as well.

The Merovingian's facility with iron increased their skill in stone work too. From all appearances, Carolingians developed a facility with slate, from roofing to siding to intricate, long cones topping towers.

Frankenbach

Ainsi-le-Franc

Not far from Karolinenfield, following the river,
is the refuge castle at Bad Berleburg amid a ring of houses
with slate siding. In this area, slate was used with abandon,

not just a touch here or there. Old entrances to slate mines can be seen along the river. This is an area that cries out for further research. In particular, it would be fascinating to

Memmingen mural on town square building, spirals on triangular roof, arcades

Ljubljana church with spirals

study the relationship between the development of slate usage between England and Germany. At a glance, it seems that this technology was broadly shared among Celts in the Iron Age, along with gold, silver, coal, salt and other mining.

The part of Charlemagne's story that seems superhuman in our jet-fast world is the scope of his presence and influence. From Carcassonne to Karlovy Vary,

139

Bad Berleburg slate house

Slate-roofed, stone church near Bad Berleburg

Charlemagne's name is exalted in one form or another. The octagon, cloisters, high columned-arched windows recall Carolingians, but mainly the place names keep Charlemagne's memory alive in Europe's mind. As with the Franks, one can only assume that it must have taken mighty forces for these remembrances to withstand the suppression and purges that have occurred since the 9th century.

Ainsi-le-Franc

Frankolova, probably former festive hall, ceiling

Lorsch Scribe with headdress in Charlemagne's Abbey

These are some names deriving from "Frank". France, Francia, Frankfurt, Frankenstein, Frankenberg, Frankolovo, Frankenwald, Franken Therme. One names that points not only to Frankish origin but also to religious take-over: Franciscan. Franciscan, for example, is the religious order associated with the Carolingian-looking building with the spirals on its pinkish-red façade in Ljubljana, Slovenia.

Romanesque – Many reasons suggest that this is a misnomer. Romanesque generally refers to a medieval style of architecture characterized by rounded arches, often of striped red and white bricks, and usually associated with the time somewhere between the 6th and 11th centuries. Towers, both domed and square, often cluster around an octagonal domed center.

Germigny-des-Près model

Ingolstadt ceiling with fountain scene. Note beheaded women

Ingolstadt - ceiling with fountain scene

Christianity is known to have taken over feast days of others as their own, like Christmas and Easter, for example, and to have used heroes venerated by others as their own, like turning the Irish Brigit into a Roman Catholic saint. Places of local significance were made into Christian churches, like the Celtic thermal baths in Jublains, France, with a church built on top of it. In that vein, convincing evidence points to Christianity having overtaken and repurposed Celtic festive halls.

Ingolstadt, Germany, city gate

Ingolstadt, a city dating back to Charlemagne's times

The octagonal hall, perfect for round banquet tables under its domed, ceiling; light-filled from the high columned-and-arched windows. The style is also commonly known as Baroque and attributed to a much later time in history.

The term Romanesque conjures up free-standing buildings, but these may have more commonly belonged to a fortified complex, like a castle or abbey. Many Merovingian and Carolingian era abbeys have been decimated, and likely by the Christian conquest. Much as the Romans felt justified in eliminating non-Roman peoples and their artifacts, Christians destroyed non-Christians as well as their buildings and belongings.

Ingolstadt (Ingold) a probable former festive hall

In the past, the lack of edifices before the 12th century has been generally attributed to barbarian attacks and the 18th century French Revolution. Almost invariably, if a historical authority talks in terms of barbarians in Europe, the blame for destruction of artifacts also falls to the barbarians. Now, though, with the advances in precision of allocating both time and causation, the ravaging of monuments can be more accurately determined. As in the case of the Flying Victory of Samothrace that graces the landing of the Louvre Museum, those who beheaded the winged female statue have been wrongly identified in the past. Now, according to museum experts, the defacement of the female statue is linked to the Christian conquest of Samothrace.

The site of 7th century Chelles Abbey, just east of Paris, is known to have been Merovingian. It is also known that Bathilde, a Merovingian female leader and freed slave, founded the abbey. What is hypothesized in this effort to establish a more factual record, is that the abbey founded by Bathilde was not religious, but secular and open to all, both men and women. Thus, when Christianity conquered Europe, the abbeys were commandeered, women excluded, and secularism banished.

Similarly, Charlemagne, his mother and sister are all said to have founded abbeys, according to Catholic records that claim the abbeys to be religious.[19, 20] Charlemagne is credited with founding 4 abbeys in the Odenwald, of which only Lorsch Abbey remains. The superb architecture with beautifully decorated façades now are undergoing restoration. In the past, barbarians and the French Revolution have been held responsible for destruction of the other 3 abbeys, but this needs to be critically reviewed through scientific means. Their destruction needs to be assessed with reference to the Christian conquest.

Deep in the heart of Charlemagne country, the town of Ingolstadt may yield valuable clues as to Carolingian style. Charles the Great reportedly referred to it as "Ingold."

Ingolstadt reflecting Carolingian Style

SHIELD WELL THE CELTIC TREASURES

Function stands with beauty
At achievement's pinnacle;
Horse and wheel, herald and shield,
Gold necklaces in the tomb.

Woven scenes with flowers and trees,
Finely clad women and men;
Castles and rivers, unicorns, bees,
Vineyards, barrels and pitchers.

The union of beauty and use -
Practicality with pleasure -
Attracts the corrupt and greedy too,
Who sabotage courage and freedom.

Rather than tribute to warriors,
Who gave their lives defending,
The golden glories go instead
To false princes, lords and kings.

Couples as heads of family
Are portrayed as kings and queens;
Lifesize panels exaulting defense
Are cast as fairy tales.

Take back the hallowed history;
Keep original memories alive.
Hold tight to life and liberty;
Let Celtic civilization thrive.

FRANKISH HEALTHCARE VILLAGES, A LASTING LEGACY

Franktiskovy Lazne thermal village, Czech lands

The Lasting Legacy of Frankish Healthcare Village Resorts

> *They bade pour out wine for the women; and seeing it was already noon, they rested there no longer, but rode till they came to broad pavilions, where they were well served. They stayed there the night through, till the early morning.*[21]

These are the words of the Nibelungenlied, a Burgundian tale of a battle with the Romans to retake their capital city of Borbetomagus, now known as Worms, Germany. It may be remembered that the Franks and Burgundians together regained

Bad Frankenhausen

Bad Frankenhausen pavilion

control of two primary strongholds that Rome had seized from
Celts, Trier being the second one. Trier on the Mosel and Worms
on the Rhine still represent the 2 major wine-producing areas
in today's Germany. These references along with additional

archeological evidence of wine throughout the Celtic Iron Age, establish a link between the Franks and wine. Another interesting tie that can be gleaned from this Nibelungenlied passage: the broad pavilions.

Pavilions still grace parks all over Europe, and pavilions and parks both associate with thermal baths. This combination of pavilion, park and thermal comes to the fore in areas known to be affiliated with the Franks, notably in the Rhineland and Slovenia. As discussed above, Karlovy Vary stands as the most heralded example of the broad pavilions, park and thermals, and it is named after the quintessential Frankish hero, Charlemagne. Others that contain "Frank" in their name provide additional information as to the importance and initiation of the wellness villages. Invariably, these self-contained, comprehensive

Park pavilion, Franktiskovy Lazne, Czech lands

Bad Frankenahausen

healthcare villages shine with stunning architecture and
resplendent parklands that hold ancient memories from ancestral
hot springs settlements.

Wintering-over was probably the most efficient way
of making it through the cold, short-day season for ancestors.
Repairing to housing clustered around hot springs turned an

Franktiskovy Lazne

Bad Frankenahausen

otherwise arduous life easy. There one could stay warm while restoring vitality in preparation for the next planting season.

It is still possible to see traces of this grand old routine. One place that triply reflects Celtic descriptive naming proclivities also feels authentically Frankish - Bad Frankenhausen, Germany. Two other essential ingredients are there too - a park and pavilion. A name like Bad Frankenhausen could not have withstood without strong forbearance, and iron will, but a remote location probably helped as well. Similarly, Franktiskovy Lazne, now in the Czech Republic, exhibits kinship with other Frankish health resorts.

Bad Kreuznach lies about halfway between Trier, where the Franks helped defeat the Romans, and Frankfurt, heart of the Celtic Rhineland. It lies in the Nahe wine district,

Franktiskovy Lazne hall

Franktosikovy Lazne, Czech lands, yellow building with white decorations

Franktiskovy Lazne cupolas and arches

midway between the Mosel and Rhine rivers. It is also the site
of a historic meeting between the leaders Charles de Gaulle
of France and Konrad Adenauer of Germany in forging the
Franco-German Alliance in 1963.

Hall by the river's vine-covered hills in Bad Kreuznach, Germany

Bad Kreuznach Parkhotel Kurhaus

"Bad" reflects its natural hot springs feature, and "Kreuznach", or "after the cross," might well refer to the fact that it lies at the mouth of the Nahe River, just a few miles before it joins the Rhine. The Rhine flows west from its source in Switzerland and turns sharply north all the way to the North Sea. Historically, this area has been a key point in the Rhine as it comes from the plains and just before it enters a long steep, high-walled canyon. It's also a place of wide slow-moving water where the Rhine can be easily crossed or circumvented.

In the former Carantania or Pannonia, many healthcare village resorts still thrive. At Bad Ischl, not far from Hallstatt after which the Iron Age period from about

RIverside dining in Parkhotel, Bad Kreuznach, Germany

Ceiling in Bad Ischl, Austria

850 to 500 B.C.E. is named, the river's edge maintains a vitality that has probably carried through from that age. A park with performance hall and pavilions also recall Celtic cultural ways.

Women, in what was almost certainly a Celtic hall before being converted into a church, are shown with their inventions in Bad Ischl, Austria. A woman riding on a cloud with an anchor –this fits into the Celtic custom of celebrating

S✢KATHARINA✢

major advancements like the wheel. Religious art obviously has been interspersed, and probably covered some of the original paintings, but the fact that some Celtic portrayals may remain deserves further attention. The portrayals of women here appear quite differently from the normal Christian portrayals of women martyrs with heads bowed and suffering. The lively spirit here typifies the old festive halls, rather than the morbid cult of death that Christianity still espouses.

A very unlikely pose for a Christian saint, here Catherine is celebrated with the wheel, decorated with a crown of gold, as a fallen defender. Amid religious overlay, signs of the zodiac and other Celtic symbols survive in this probable former fest hall.

CONCLUSION

Lady and the Unicorn Tapestry, Museum of the Middle Ages, Paris, France

Conclusion

Francia still lives through the Franks. France could not have retained its name, were it not for the strength and valor of the Frankish family of Celts. The name "Frank" harkens back to the ideals of a people, themselves struggling to remain free while coming to the aid of relatives under attack.

Uncovering Europe's Celtic past can bring its present into clearer focus, so that the world can see a more accurate ancestral story. By knowing family stories, a truer picture of Celtic Europe can emerge and lead to a future of liberty and justice for all. These are the key values of a free world; they are not about conquest, but about fairness and equality, where men, women and children play their natural leading roles in the direction and balance of society. Give credit where credit is due, beginning with the role of Franks in freedom.

IT'S TIME TO BRING BACK THE BALANCE & BEAUTY THAT OUR ANCESTORS CHERISHED & GUARDED.

ENDNOTES

1. The Pannonian Basin is also known as the Carpathian Basin, long ascribed as the homeland of the Slavs. "Slav," it may be remembered, has been used synonymously with "slave" by imperial rulers, and may well mean only that. Linguistic fictions run rampant through the Byzantine era.

2. Rajko Bratož, ur., Slovenija in sosednje dežele med antiko in karolinško dobo : začetki slovenske etnogeneze = Slowenien und die Nachbarländer zwischen Antike und karolingischer Epoche : Anfänge der slowenischen Ethnogenese, 2 zv. Ljubljana, 2000. See also Bogo Grafenauer, Ustoličevanje koroških vojvod in država karantanskih Slovencev: Die Kärntner Herzogseinsetzung und der Staat der Karantanerslawen. Ljubljana, 1952.

3. As a reminder, the Hidden Women series adopts the core theory that Franks and Burgundians were among Europe's Iron Age resident families. Celts notoriously came to each other's aid to fend off Roman attacks, like when Vercingetorix of Auvergne helped the Burgundians fight Julius Caesar in Alesia. For a fuller explanation, the reader is invited to review the first two books in the series, available gratis in e-form on the Hiddenwomenbooks.com website.

4. Goldberg, Eric J. *Struggle for Empire: Kingship and Conflict under Louis the German 817-876*, Cornell, Cornell University Press, 2006

5. Feudalism means a master-servant regime in which royalty owns all the people and all the land. Series), Peabody Museum Press, Cambridge, 2006.

6. Wells, Spencer, *The Journey of Man: A Genetic Odyssey* (Princeton Science Library), Princeton University Press, Princeton, N. J., 2017

7. Please see the first two books in the Hidden Women series for further discussion of Celts, women and wine.

8. Greis, Gloria Polizzotti, *A Noble Pursuit: The Duchess of Mecklenburg Collection from Iron Age Slovenia* (Peabody Collection Series), Harvard Press, Cambridge, 2006.

9. See generally Wikipedia, Bamberg witch trials. https://en.wikipedia.org/wiki/Bamberg_witch_trials

10. https://en.wikipedia.org/wiki/Walpurgis_Night. Abbess Walpurgis.

11. https://de.wikipedia.org/wiki/Abenberg re Abbess Stille.

12. Nixey, Catherine, *The Darkening Age: The Christian Destruction of the Classical World*, Houghton, Miflin, Harcourt, Boston, 2017.

13. Chicago, Judy. *The Dinner Party*, Monicelli Press, New York. 2014.

14. "Gregory of Tours was the first to have mentioned the element that has shaped subsequent interpretations of Tolbiac as a climactic in European history: Clovis is said to have attributed his success to a vow that he had made: if he won, he would convert to the religion of the Christian God who had aided him. He became a Christian in a ceremony at Reims at Christmas 496. [3] The traditional date of the battle of Tolbiac has been established to accord with this firmly attested baptismal date, by accepting Gregory's account. A surviving letter from Avitus of Vienne, congratulating Clovis on his

baptism, makes no mention of the supposed recent battlefield conversion.[4]" https://en.wikipedia.org/wiki/Battle_of_Tolbiac

15. Buri, Rapp, Anna and Monica Stucky-Schürer, *Burgundische Tapisserien*, Hirmer Publishers, Munich, 2001.

16. Buri, Rapp, Anna and Monica Stucky-Schürer, Burgundische Tapisserien, supra.

17. Krebs, Christopher B., *A Most Dangerous Book: Tacitus's Germania from the Roman Empire to the Third Reich*, New York, W. W. Norton & Company, 2012.

18. Barraclough, *The Origins of Modern Germany*, 263.

19. Chicago, Judy. *The Dinner Party*, Monicelli Press, New York. 2014.

20. Chicago, Judy. *The Dinner Party*, Monicelli Press, New York. 2014.

21. http://www.fullbooks.com/The-Fall-of-the-Niebelungs3.html 21st Adventure.FullBooks.com

BIBLIOGRAPHY

Archäologie zwischen Donnersberg und Worms: Ausflüge in ein altes Kulturland, Verlag Schnell & Steiner, Regensburg, 2008

Barraclough, Geoffrey, *The Origins of Modern Germany*, W.W.Norton & Company, New York City, 1984

Blockmans, Wim, and Walter Prevnier, *The Promised Lands: The Low Countries Under Burgundian Rule, 1369 – 1530*, Translated by Elizabeth Fakelman. Philadelphia, University of Pennsylvania Press, 1999.

Bratož, Rajko, ur., Slovenija in sosednje dežele med antiko in karolinško dobo : začetki slovenske etnogeneze = Slowenien und die Nachbarländer zwischen Antike und karolingischer Epoche : Anfänge der slowenischen Ethnogenese, 2 zv. Ljubljana, 2000. See also Bogo Grafenauer, Ustoličevanje koroških vojvod in država karantanskih Slovencev : Die Kärntner Herzogseinsetzung und der Staat der Karantanerslawen.Ljubljana, 1952.

Buri, Rapp, Anna and Monica Stucky-Schürer, *Burgundische Tapisserien*, Hirmer Publishers, Munich, 2001

Chicago, Judy. *The Dinner Party*, Monicelli Press, New York. 2014.

De la Tours, Gregory, *The History of the Franks*, attributed to 5th century, republished by Penguin Groups, London, 1974.

Goldberg, Eric J. *Struggle for Empire: Kingship and Conflict under Louis the German 817-876*, Ithaca, Cornell University Press, 2006.

Greis, Gloria Polizzotti, *A Noble Pursuit: The Duchess of Mecklenburg Collection from Iron Age Slovenia* (Peabody Collection Series), Harvard Press, Cambridge, 2006.

Jones, Terry and Alan Ereira, *Barbarians: An Alternative Roman History*, Ebony Publishing, a Division of Random House, Oxford, from the movie the Barbarians by the BBC.

Krebs, Christopher B., *A Most Dangerous Book: Tacitus's Germania from the Roman Empire to the Third Reich*, New York, W. W. Norton & Company, 2012.

Nixey, Catherine, *The Darkening Age: The Christian Destruction of the Classical World*, Houghton, Miflin, Harcourt, Boston, 2017.

Robb, Graham, *The Discovery of Middle Earth: Mapping the Lost World of the Celts*, W.W. Norton & Company, New York, 2013.

Wells, Spencer, *The Journey of Man: A Genetic Odyssey* (Princeton Science Library), Princeton University Press, Princeton, N. J., 2017

Wikipedia, internet encyclopedia, hosted by Wikimedia Foundation, a non-profit organization.

APPENDIX

WATCH FOR CELTIC WORDS

If a name sounds Celtic, look for other indications of Celtic presence.

One general premise that we use is that Celtic ways are handed down from generation to generation. Ways of describing and naming can come through regardless of what particular language is being used. Basic geographical descriptions helpful to orienting the travelers have persisted through the ages.

For example, In Slovenia, high and low *–gor, gora, gorica*, and *dol – Dole, dolina* - are used often. In Germany it's *berg* at the end of words, and words like *nieder under ober* (lower and upper) as prefixes. *Berg* means hilltop or mountain; *feld* means field; lowland is *Niederland*, highland is *Hochland*.

Gart or *jard* - means both park and garden, as in *Le Grand Jard City Park* in Chalons-en-Champagne, France.

Hall - Old English hall, *heall* (originally denoting a roofed space, located centrally, for the communal use. From Great Britain to Central Europe, the word hall can be found to mean a grand gathering enclosure with high painted ceilings and highly crafted woodwork. The hall can be showcased as the literal hallmark of a town or city, obvious by "hall" in its name, as in *Hallstatt, Hallein, Halle, Schwäbisch Hall.*

Kirk, Kirche - the later word, église, added the element of religion, or ecclesiastic

Pavillon – open-air structure with roof and pillars. Karlovy Vary, the Czech Republic, serves as a grand example. Simpler ones can offer food and shelter in the woords like the *Pavilion de la Fontaine* in Luxembourg Gardens in Paris, and the *Pavilion at the Kurhaus.*

Bath, bain or *had* – also *therme*   means hot springs when used in a place name. *Baden-Baden, Bad Ischl, Salins-les-Bains.* In Slavic-speaking lands, the term is "*toplice*" or a form thereof. Current usage now includes residential bathing rooms.

Abbey, Abbaye, Kloster – a self-contained center of learning and production; precursor to the university.

Basilica – gathering place, in the Greek language.

Hilltop fort – *oppidum* (Latin), *dunum* (Celtic)

Hof, commanderie – a farm complex that faces inward toward a center courtyard, with the buildings connecting and acting as a perimeter wall. The town of Hof in

Chateau, castle, castrum, fortress Burg, grad, furt, – fortified, surrounded by a moat, affords refuge to residents of surrounding area when under attack; set up to provide safety and sustenance over long periods of time.

Chapeau – chapelle – men's and women's hatrooms in former festive halls – literally. Same vintage as the cloak room.

Dom – home, domain - probably later adopted the meaning of cathedral

FRANK
TALK

EXALTING WHAT NOW?

Taught to be subservient
Taught to be contrite
Taught to be obedient
Believe with all your might

"Such fun, eternal slavery
Can't wait for kingdom come
When all we'll do is carry out
The master's word, and then some."

Praise a god whose son has died -
His father made it happen;
And if you fail to toe the line,
You'll see the same with your son,

Sit in former festive halls
That used to ring with laughter.
Fear the everlasting pain -
Fear the ever-after.

"Unending doom is yours unless
You give your all to us.
Don't bother understanding it
Just leave your brain with us."

Wait, what – your god committed infanticide?
Isn't that barbaric?

IN CONVERSATION
WITH THE AUTHOR

Religion's not so bad, is it? It provides community and comfort.

Those side aspects are fine, but you don't need religion to do that. Join a sports or service club. My objection is the feudalism – the lord and master subservience with blind obedience that allows no independent thinking.

What does it hurt to believe in something you can't see? It hurts because it leads so easily to fraud. Proving loyalty often belongs to mafia-type initiation processes that go awry. If this unseen god sacrificed his son, why wouldn't he expect the same of followers, and punish anyone who dared disappoint. Reasonable people ordinarily shun such dark subjects, but not when they're part of religious doctrine.

Just because Christian deities don't include women doesn't equate to sexism, does it?

It doesn't stop with father-son gods who lack mother-daughter goddesses. It extends to the language and the imagery. Churches glorify men and vilify women.   It's in the liturgy, the story and the portrayals.

Men bow down in religion as much as women. Where's the problem?

Think about the difference between a great hall for celebrating and a church. In churches it's common for women to be depicted as contrite, sometimes even holding a dead son. When do you ever see the father god holding a dead son? It's a message to women in particular – step out of line and we'll kill your family.

What's wrong with communion? It's just a ritual that brings people together.

Think about it. What is the symbolism of eating and drinking human flesh and blood? Isn't this showing subservience? Even if it is interpreted as gaining attributes by ingesting them, is this a charade that thinking people want to do? Isn't it just peer pressure that makes people go to the front of the room and participate in pretend cannibalism?

How can we know that any Celts survived?

They were too numerous and widespread for Roman and successor empires to have eradicated them completely. Looking at the inclinations of most Europeans, it's impossible to ignore the core Celtic stewardship that continues to exist. Most people don't take concubines, nor do they want to damage the environment or torture those who don't agree with them. The hospitality and generosity of Celts lives on in perceivable ways right along with the devotion to nature and family.

Praying to a deity for redemption is just an exercise in humility. No harm in that, is there?

Isn't the Christian belief that Christ died for your sins, but then rose again? If he rose again, he's not dead. Why should anyone 2000 years later feel responsible for a death that was obviated? People who consider themselves Christian needs to confront this. It doesn't make any sense.

Are you saying that Celtic women have been targeted? Weren't the men slaughtered too?

Romans slaughtered both men and women as part of their military campaign to gain control of Celtic Europe. Their strategy of attacking women was to weaken the pillar of Celtic society, the family. Celts revered women as uniquely equipped to bear and nurture the children, but this also rendered females more vulnerable. Molesting and enslaving women and children brought the men to their knees. Evidence suggests more and more that Celtic people spent a lot of time and brainpower hiding and protecting their women and children.

Rome still means all-male hierarchy.

INDEX

The author, Jacqueline Widmar Stewart

AUTHOR
INSIGHTS

What vistas opened up when we looked underground!

Now, with each European trip our new lens gives my husband Blair and me ever more astonishing views of Celts. The more we look, the more we see a rich, flourishing world where women play a vital role.

Standing in archaeological sites allows one a sense of the past in incomparable ways. There you can walk in the steps of ancestral Celts and see what they saw. Invariably, the river still burbles over the rocks and the breezes blow across the mountain in the same directions.

Two strains from the Celtic Iron Age remain vibrant in my family and I prize them above all: the preeminence of children and the stewardship of the natural world. That is why the Iron Age feels so familiar to me and impassions me to learn more. My time spent in Slovenia puts me in touch with the ancient past in ways that are very tangible - from the thermal baths, to the inns in the forests, to the ubiquitous need to visit the river's source.

Thinking back, I can identify Celtic ideals throughout my life. From earliest childhood I was fortunate to have parents who, despite their own limited elementary school training, put the education of their 3 daughters as their top priority. As a result, I have studied at universities in Slovenia and Germany, as well as Stanford, Michigan and Colorado.

My grandparents had immigrated from the Austro-Hungarian Empire before the start of World War I. What drove them to leave a place of such unparalleled natural grandeur has driven me to understand what happened in Europe. Studies of conventional history have rung far too fabricated to be true.

Greatest revelations have come from the very first entry we made into the European homeland. As soon as my parents and I set out to find long-lost relatives during my spring break from the university in Bonn, enigmas quickly piled up in our way. How could our European family have been sliced into different ethnicities, nationalities, religions, and language-speakers in the space of just one generation?

Our newfound Austrian and Yugoslavian relatives could not have been more different – or more the same. It was as though they had been kidnapped them to warring planets, yet they shared such obvious commonalities. We felt an immediate kinship to those on both sides of the border. How could insurmountable barriers have been erected between the two, and so fast!

It felt so wrong to be speaking German to Slovenian relatives when they had learned it only because of their displacement to Germany during World War II. I wanted to learn Slovenian no matter what! It took me a while to realize that no one in the US was teaching Slovenian at the time, but things worked out sublimely when I landed at the University in Ljubljana for a year to learn it.

My fragmented pursuit of this study in some odd way reflects the fragmented aspects of European history. Whether trying to track tapestry studios in Flanders or probing the meaning of paganism, I have run into so many brick walls. It has taken years of perking and drawing lines that sometimes work and sometimes don't, but I wouldn't trade anything for my "ah-ha" moments.

In retrospect, the pieces of my life that seemed so disjointed actually have made these discoveries possible. Slovenian grandparents, our tapestry-import business, the study of law, conversance with language, education, parks and gardens, champagne, Lake Michigan – equipped with special perspectives like these we have been able to see a most beautiful Celtic pentimento emerging from under the countless layers that have covered it.

Many years ago, my legal career focused on women's rights, and there has been a big hiatus in picking up that thread again. In between times, I concentrated on issues of environment and education. These facets of experience, too, have helped broaden the field of vision.

A more recent thread from my past weaves into the present through the efforts of the immensely talented graphics designer, Remy Steiner. Thankfully, she is also possessed of a pioneering spirit. The first book The Glaciers' Treasure Trove gave us a crash course in publishing and now the HIDDEN WOMEN books are plunging us headlong into the digital age. I stand in awe of her triumphs over technology, but also the beauty of her work and her tenacity in producing it. Please visit our hiddenwomenbooks.com website to see what I mean. Her stunning work befits the Celts.

Our wish for readers: May you find these materials so timely and intriguing that you join this quest to decipher Europe's secret past. Help restore Celtic equilibrium and fairness to a troubled world.

HIDDEN
WOMEN

A History of Europe
Celts & Freedom

by Jacqueline Widmar Stewart

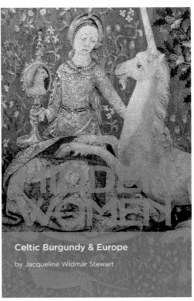

HIDDEN
WOMEN

Celtic Burgundy & Europe

by Jacqueline Widmar Stewart

HIDDEN WOMEN BOOKS SERIES OVERVIEW

As an on-going exploration, this study seeks to gain insights into the present from Europe's buried past. A century ago, a woman in Slovenia began uncovering artifacts that challenged history's conventional telling, and today archeologists are adding to this body of knowledge across the continent and British Isles.

It is becoming increasingly clear that the pre-Christians revered women as the gateway to the future, but also honored the leadership, valor and accomplishments of both their men and women. The unavoidable conclusion is that a dramatic change in the treatment of women has occurred during the past 2500 years. By identifying and addressing the causes for this deterioration, equilibrium can return. A deeper understanding of ancestral Celts portends to strengthen the foundations of current society, and especially the family.

The first book in the HIDDEN WOMEN series, *A History of Europe, Celts and Freedom*, gives a broad, general introduction to the topic. Later volumes delve into various aspects of Celtic Europe to gain a more comprehensive vie of the entirety. Given the immensity of the subject matter, a major goal of this project is to engender more research by others. Please help.

Made in the USA
Monee, IL
06 March 2023

29250010R00121